W9-ANP-640

A IS FOR AFRICA

Thanks to Emily, my mother, and all my family for encouraging me.
Thanks to Roger for his help, and to Emeka for inspiring me.

PUFFIN BOOKS
Published by the Penguin Group
Penguin Putnam Books for Young Readers, 345 Hudson Street, New York, New York 10014, U.S.A.
Penguin Books Ltd, 27 Wrights Lane, London W8 5TZ, England
Penguin Books Australia Ltd, Ringwood, Victoria, Australia
Penguin Books Canada Ltd, 10 Alcorn Avenue, Toronto, Ontario, Canada M4V 3B2
Penguin Books (N.Z.) Ltd, 182-190 Wairau Road, Auckland 10, New Zealand

Penguin Books Ltd, Registered Offices: Harmondsworth, Middlesex, England

Originally published in Great Britain by Frances Lincoln Limited, 1993
First published in the United States of America by Cobblehill Books,
an affiliate of Dutton Children's Books, a division of Penguin Books USA Inc., 1993
Published in Puffin Books, 1997

29 30

Text and photographs copyright © Ifeoma Onyefulu, 1993
All rights reserved

THE LIBRARY OF CONGRESS HAS CATALOGED THE COBBLEHILL EDITION AS FOLLOWS:
Onyefulu, Ifeoma
A is for Africa / Ifeoma Onyefulu. p. cm.
Summary: The author, a member of the Igbo tribe in Nigeria, presents text and her own photographs
of twenty-six things, from A to Z, representatives of all African peoples.
ISBN 0-525-65147-0
1. Africa—Juvenile literature. 2. English language—Alphabet—Juvenile literature.
[1. Africa. 2. Alphabet.] I. Title.
DT3.159 1993 960-dc20 [E] 92-39964 CIP AC

Puffin Books ISBN 978-0-14-056222-4

Designed by Patricia Howes.
The self-ends are based on a textile design by Chinye Onyefulu.

Manufactured in China

A IS FOR AFRICA

Ifeoma Onyefulu

Puffin Books

A Note from the Author

This alphabet is based on my own favorite images of the Africa I know. I come from the Igbo tribe and grew up in southeastern Nigeria. It was in Nigeria that these photographs were taken, but the people and things pictured reflect the rich diversity of the continent as a whole.

There are examples of Moslem and Arabic influences from the north of my country, as well as costumes and ornaments from the south where the religions are animist or Christian. These religions are found in other African countries, too. There are kola nuts, indigo, and beaded jewelry and the ways in which Nigerians use them. And though other Africans may use a different kind of nut, a different color dye, and jewelry that looks different, the meanings and customs associated with them are the same.

I wanted to capture what the people of Africa have in common: traditional village life, warm family ties, and above all, the hospitality for which Africans are famous. This book shows what Africa is to me, but it is for and about all the peoples of this vast, friendly, colorful continent.

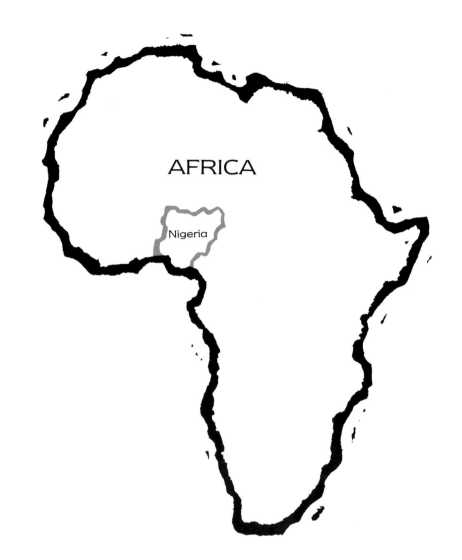

AFRICA

Nigeria

 is for Africa, a great continent of many countries and peoples. The African people come from large families called tribes. They may dress differently and speak different languages, but Africa is home to them all.

Bb

is for the Beads a girl may wear on her head, ears, or neck. They come in lots of different shapes, sizes, and colors – red, green, blue, and yellow.

is for a Canoe to paddle down the river. Canoes are used for fishing and carrying goods to market. People may visit their friends or take their children to school by canoe.

Dd is for the Drums used to make music and announce special meetings and important news in many villages. When a newborn baby is named, relatives and friends may welcome him or her into the world with the sound of drums.

Ee

is the Embrace we give our loved ones. Africans are very warm people, and this is how they welcome relatives and friends. They embrace to show their happiness and give each other support. Dancers embrace at the end of a performance.

Ff

is for the Feathers a chief wears on his hat. Hats and feathers are handed down from father to son, when the son reaches middle age. This Igbo chief's feathers are from the eagle. In this tribe, women can be chiefs too, but they don't wear feathers.

Gg is for Grandmother, telling wonderful stories about animals and people that lived long ago. She is a very special person in family life.

Hh

is for mud Houses, just right for a hot climate. Most places in Africa are hot during the day and cool at night. In the daytime, the mud walls keep out the hot sunshine. At night the mud bricks release the heat they have absorbed during the day and warm the inside of the house.

 is for Indigo, a blue powder from the indigo plant that is used to dye clothes. A good way to dye cloth is to leave it to soak in a mixture of powder and water in a very deep hole in the ground. Letting the cloth dry in the open air helps set the color.

is for Jumping with the other children in the village. In the evenings when the sun is setting, children gather to play. Jumping over sticks is a favorite game.

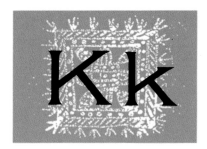

Kk

is for Kola nuts offered to guests to show warmth and friendship. The nuts grow in pods on tall trees, and they keep well after they have been picked. In many parts of Africa, on an important occasion, old men and women may say prayers and the oldest man present breaks the kola nuts.

Ll

is for Lamps. Some homemade lamps are made of clay, but these are used milk-tins. They have wicks to burn oil, paraffin, or kerosene.

Mm

is for Masquerade, a mask and costume made to honor the spirit of an ancestor. They are sacred objects, brought out only for special occasions. The artists chosen to make masquerades spend months designing them before they show them in public.

 is for Neighbors, passing on the latest news.

is for Ornaments to adorn our bodies. African people love to dress up and look beautiful. In some tribes people wear beaded strands around their waists or across their chests. Body markings are another kind of ornament.

 **Pp** is for earthenware Pots, for storing water and keeping it cool. They give the water a fresh, earthy taste. Women sometimes use a pot as a musical instrument, beating it to give out a very deep sound.

Qq

is for Queen, wearing her crown and splendid jewelry. Not so long ago, there were lots of powerful kings and queens in Africa, but nowadays there are only a few.

is for River. Africans believe many rivers are sacred. In villages, they take care to keep their river clean, and they set aside special areas for fishing, washing, and swimming.

Ss is for Shaking hands. Children and grown-ups shake hands when they meet friends or relatives. When two Igbo chiefs shake hands they use the back of the hand, not the front, to show how important they are. Young men and women raise and clasp hands with their friends at big gatherings.

Tt

is for Turban. A Muslim man may wear this special turban if he is very knowledgeable about the Islamic religion and has visited Mecca, the holy center of Islam. Women may also wear turbans to help them carry heavy loads on their heads.

Uu

is for Umbrella, even better than a big leaf for giving shelter from the hot sun. A mother may use an umbrella to shade a new baby, and market traders will use one to keep their goods from wilting in the sun.

is for the Village, where many people live together, sharing the same traditions and beliefs. The old people in the village teach the young ones the old customs, as they were once taught themselves.

 is for Weaving. Some tribes weave their own fabrics from locally produced cotton. Parents teach the craft to their children. Each region has its own story of how weaving began.

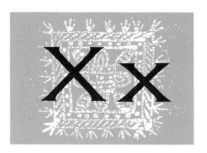

is for the Xylophone many villages use in their music. It is made from wood that gives a beautiful sound. Each key is a different length and makes a different note when the player strikes it.

is for the Yams that grow in our gardens. They are like potatoes, but yams are bigger and take longer to grow. We boil yams or roast them and eat them with palm oil. Either way, they taste delicious.

 is the rough Zigzag lane leading to my village.
And that's the end.